48-75

PRIVATE
ROME

Publisher *Beatrice Vincenzini*
Editorial Director *Alexandra Black*
Project Manager *David Shannon*
Art Director *David Mackintosh*
Design *Pentrix Design*
Project Coordinator *Emma Bini*
Publishing Assistant *Emma Head*

Colour Reproduction *Bright Arts, Singapore*

Published in the UK by Scriptum Editions
Created by Co & Bear Productions (UK) Ltd.

Printed and bound in Novara, Italy by Officine Grafiche de Agostini
First edition
10 9 8 7 6 5 4 3 2 1
ISBN 0–9527665–5–8

PRIVATE
ROME

PHOTOGRAPHY BY FRANCESCO VENTURI
WRITTEN BY ELIZABETH HELMAN MINCHILLI

SCRIPTUM EDITIONS

LONDON · HONG KONG

CONTENTS

PREFACE

I.

STUDIOS

12

OPPOSITE AND LEFT

Giancarlo Giammetti's office was perhaps the most difficult room to resolve when Valentino decided to redecorate his headquarters in Palazzo Mignanelli. The coffered, frescoed ceiling of what was once the grand salon of the palace dwarfed every piece of furniture that was brought in. The designer's solution was to unify the vast space through art, displaying Giammetti's extensive collection of paintings, sculpture and art deco furniture. The final effect is more akin to a gallery than a businessman's office.

OPPOSITE, LEFT, AND BELOW
The London-based firm of David Davis Associates designed the sleek first floor offices, studios and changing rooms as a backdrop for both Valentino's designs and art collection. The large painting in the corridor is by Fernando Botero, and the slim figure in white Carrara marble is an Italian sculpture from the late nineteenth century.

OPPOSITE

Valentino's personal refuge is covered in a hand-painted wallpaper. The pattern is reproduced from a fabric that appears in a portrait of Eleanor Toledo by the Florentine mannerist Angelo Bronzino. A nineteenth-century eclecticism prevails throughout the room, with rich gilt surfaces running up against bright checks and bold leopard prints. The beautifully framed still life is a seventeenth-century work by Christian Berentz.

LEFT

A nineteenth-century marble lion nestles on the mantlepiece in Valentino's office. A photograph of a pair of hands sits behind, inspired by a Roger Duncan sketch and used as the key image in the thirtieth-birthday celebrations of the design house.

INTERIOR STAGING

IT IS NOT SURPRISING THAT DESIGNER VERDE VISCONTI views her interiors as a sort of stage set, with each person playing a role and each having their own entrances. One of her earliest memories is of a theatre production put on by her cousin, director Luchino Visconti. At age seven she was already impressed by the dramatic possibilities within a few sheets of gauze floating in the breeze.

Unlike others in her trade Visconti does not claim to have a signature style. Instead she insists on long interviews to uncover her clients' personalities. The quirky, personal traits of the owners become the overriding theme in her interior creations. Her rooms are classic, yet with a strong, Zen-like simplicity. She has an eye for interesting details, and for elements which define and delineate space, such as floors, frames and doors.

Visconti views travel as a chance to look for new fabrics to use in her designs. She sees fabrics as the concrete expression of other civilizations and ancient artisanal traditions, and within her environments she mixes shot silk with rough, hand-loomed cottons. It is as much the colours as the varied textures that she uses to create warmth and comfort.

After working as a buyer for Bergdorf Goodman and as an assistant to designer John Stefanidis in London, Visconti finally returned to Rome where she worked with Stefano Mantovani for eight years. She eventually opened her own office, up the street from the Spanish Steps, and counts among her most recent clients Nicola Bulgari and Leonardo Mondadori. Her small suite of offices is telling of her style: simple, spare, yet filled with hand-picked objects which reflect their owner's taste and personality.

RESTORATION EFFECTS

OPPOSITE AND ABOVE

Ilaria Miani's ground floor space is half workshop, half showroom. Frames hang by the dozen on wall pegs; more are stacked around the floor or stored on shelves alongside piles of materials for fashioning lamps, trays or furniture. Finishing touches are applied on a large work table. When not in use, it serves as a display area for Miani's favourite items.

SINCE ROMAN TIMES, the neighbourhood known as Trastevere, literally 'across the Tiber River', has been the city's playground, located near enough to the protective walls to allow Rome's inhabitants a quick escape to hunting lodges, pleasure pavilions and gardens. While most of the area is now as built up as the rest of the city, there is part that has escaped development and retains its intensely green character. It is here that Ilaria Miani lives with her family in a small seventeenth-century house, originally the stables of Cardinal d'Alibert whose villa stands close by amid a field of wild flowers.

When Miani first discovered the building, it seemed tailor-made for her newly formed business. She could live upstairs with her husband, using the level below for her workshop. Trained as an art historian, Miani spent several years working in various galleries before starting her own venture producing custom-made picture frames and furniture.

The ground floor is now a showroom for her extensive line of handcrafted wooden furnishings. Mostly small-scale, the items are all collapsible. Folding chairs and tables, expandable bookshelves and portable trays fill the light-drenched space. Most are reproductions of classic eighteenth- and nineteenth-century designs, yet they have the unique quality of a handmade object and the patina of an antique.

Her private apartment upstairs is the perfect testing ground for her designs. In the living room, echoing the classical beauty of an ancient Roman map that covers one entire wall, circular side tables are draped in cloths to form pedestals for clusters of pretty gilt frames and her signature standing lamps with their subtly textured shades.

RIGHT ·

Miani's home is full of her own creations.
A towel rack and tiered shelves are put to use
in the master bathroom, where the combination
of wooden furnishings with framed prints, a
comfortable arm-chair and paved floor creates
a charming, old-world atmosphere.

OPPOSITE

When Miani first opened her shop, the emphasis
was on creative frames. While these still make up
a good proportion of her production, folding chairs
and tables have also been added to the line.

OPPOSITE AND ABOVE

Sunlight drenches Miani's rooftop living room, which is fully glazed along two walls and looks out onto a garden terrace. Eschewing traditional wallpapers, Miani chose instead to cover the principal wall with a reproduction sixteenth-century map of Rome. The colour scheme of maroon and gold was copied from a favourite nineteenth-century painting of an interior, but Miani added a modern touch with a pair of boldly striped black and white sofas. Many of the side tables and lamps are designed by her.

THE COSTUMER'S ART

IN THE RELATIVELY SHORT SPACE OF THIRTY YEARS, Tirelli Costumi has become an Italian legend. Tucked away in Rome's Prati neighbourhood, a few blocks away from the Vatican, the costume house employs a handful of artisans crafting some of the world's most extravagant clothing for film, opera and theatre. It is the brainchild of Umberto Tirelli, who launched the venture by creating costumes for two of Italy's best-known film directors of the 1960s, Luchino Visconti and Federico Fellini. Films to Tirelli's credit now number over sixty, many of them Oscar winners including *The English Patient* and *The Age of Innocence*.

Much of the film world's fascination with the costume house is a consequence of Umberto Tirelli's passion for antique apparel. Fuelled by this obsession, the firm has built up a collection of well over fifteen thousand accessories and items of clothing, spanning the last four hundred years of dress design. Meticulously preserved, the archive of costumes provides a rich resource for fashion historians and designers alike.

Now following in the footsteps of Tirelli, his associate, Dino Trappetti, continues the tradition of welcoming costume designers from around the globe. Hollywood designer Ruth Carter chose the Roman studio to breathe life into her ideas for Steven Spielberg's *Amistad*. Deborah Scott's designs for James Cameron's *Titanic* were also crafted here. So while the heyday of Italian cinema is only a memory, the international film community keeps Tirelli Costumi's scores of seamstresses and embroiderers working at full pace. Fittingly, after their long voyages to distant sets, the costumes return home to remain part of the studio's historic archive.

ABOVE

*Every corner of the Tirelli studios reveals new surprises that recall the grandeur
of period dress. This white Edwardian-style gown was worn by Winona Ryder
in Martin Scorsese's 1994 film* The Age Of Innocence, *for which costume
designer Gabriella Pescucci won an Oscar.*

RIGHT

*Trappetti's office creates an air of turn-of-the-century romance with its
solid, antique furnishings, walls filled with framed sketches and illustrations,
and clusters of mementos, all relating to the proud history of Tirelli Costumi.*

RIGHT AND OPPOSITE

Among the keepsakes in Dino Trappetti's office
are portraits of former partner and founder of
the studio, Umberto Tirelli. Despite the apparent
clutter of objects, room is made for a mannequin
clad in a rich red velvet housecoat, worn by
Michelle Pfeiffer in The Age of Innocence.

SCULPTURAL PRECISION

THE SELF-CONTAINED WORLD OF SCULPTOR MARIO CEROLI is enclosed behind a front gate patterned with hundreds of small pine pyramids, weathered to a soft silvery grey. Beyond it, a black and white marble-paved courtyard serves as a formal welcome in this otherwise bucolic landscape. Olive trees and umbrella pines provide the setting for the artist's outdoor works, while several rustic buildings make up working and living spaces.

In the large and luminous warehouse-like spaces he has erected, Ceroli has chosen to create a series of galleries for his sculptures, rather than storing them in crates, or stacking them up against each other in cramped quarters. Lofty sky-lit ceilings and sweeping expanses of white wall form the background to a constantly expanding and changing exhibit. Although in reality all is static, there is a constant sense of movement. Horses, human figures, even the natural elements seem caught in motion by Ceroli's hand. Some of the images are familiar and have become national symbols, such as the rearing horse Ceroli originated for the national broadcast company RAI. Other works are more elusive, such as the twelve-foot-long glass wave, massive in its proportions yet strangely poetic in its silence.

That Ceroli lives in a world of his own is confirmed by the distinctive character of his living area with its fluid forms and warm, natural tones. The sharp, sculptural lines of the wood furnishings are balanced by the broad curve of the internal arches and windows. Solid shapes of rough-hewn wood and stone are softened by pristine white upholstery, walls and ceilings. Every object, from lamp to table to chair, has been designed and crafted by the sculptor to fulfil a unique artistic vision.

ABOVE

Ceroli's fireplace, built from brick, recalls the Renaissance monsters in the garden at Bomarzo.

RIGHT AND OPPOSITE

Every element in the home – including tables, chairs, couches, lamps, even radiator covers – has been designed by Ceroli to create a soothing and spacious environment characterized by warm wood tones and sculptural shapes.

ABOVE AND RIGHT

Although he is best known for his work in wood, Ceroli is just as comfortable sculpting from layered sheets of glass. He uses the glass in much the same way as he does timber, building up massive rounded shapes from hundreds of individual, two-dimensional planes. The glass thereby loses its transparency, taking on instead a deep green opacity.

FAR LEFT

*Ceroli's work is as much about process as
it is about the finished product or piece of art.
This project in his studio explores the abstract
and literal idea of following one's own road.*

LEFT, ABOVE AND BELOW

*Giant stone and wood pendulums hang from
the rafters of the artist's warehouse, while three
glass spirals, entitled 'Tree of Life', soar skywards.*

41

OPPOSITE, LEFT, AND BELOW

The most formal part of the compound is the entrance court, which includes a large swimming pool. Dubbed 'Piazza d'Italia' by the artist, it is a graphic study in black and white, and explores concepts of perspective and pattern.

43

II.

APARTMENTS

PRIMARY PALETTE

OPPOSITE AND ABOVE

Nina von Fürstenberg designed the ottoman in the living room using lengths of velvet brought back from Oman. The modern Persian rug, which picks out the primary tones of the rest of the room, was a lucky find from a dealer in Zurich. The artworks chosen for the room also echo the bold colour scheme, including a trio of small works by Alighiero Boetti, hung together on the red wall.

WANDERING THE STREETS OF ROME'S working class neighbourhood Trastevere, Nina von Fürstenberg lit upon the perfect place to settle down and raise her family with husband Angelo Bucarelli. The apartment she fell for, in a small sixteenth-century building on the Via Garibaldi, would need complete reworking to suit the couple's particular tastes, but their first task was convincing the owners to sell. After much negotiation the sale went through, and the transformation process began.

Once the couple had settled on a workable floor plan, they set about choosing the interior scheme that now defines the mood of their home. The emotive power of colour, in which Angelo Bucarelli firmly believes, is the major decorating device in the apartment. Strong primary colours mark the living room, with three walls painted red, blue and yellow. The existing arched ceilings lend graceful definition to the wide expanses of saturated colour, turning the walls into a three-panelled minimalist painting. This dramatic use of colour and shape extends to the all-white dining room, which is separated from the living area by a large curved panel on wheels.

As both Bucarelli and von Fürstenberg have such strong ideas, they prefer to craft objects and furnishing elements themselves rather than call in local artisans, often using materials found on their travels in far-flung places. A screen in the children's room is constructed out of a simple frame and remnants picked up in London; bright velvets from Oman have been fashioned into an ottoman; lengths of transparent orange polyester gauze are crafted into glowing curtains; and Tricia Guild fabrics picked up in London seem to speak the same boldly coloured language they do.

RIGHT

Red, yellow and blue define the three arched walls of the living room, serving as a backdrop for the couple's ever-expanding and changing art collection. The sofas are in more muted shades, balancing the strong walls and lending focus to the bright ottoman in the centre of the room.

OPPOSITE

The sitting room is the heart of the apartment, its archways opening out to the living room, dining room and the master bedroom. A pair of windows flanking the fireplace make this the sunniest room in the house. The black and white curtain rods were von Fürstenberg's invention – using wooden dowels and black electrician's tape, she created a strong graphic support for the hot orange drapery.

LEFT

A rare original set of Fornasetti plates from the 1950s make an eye-catching display with their gold and white glazes. Colour is used to highlight here rather than dominate as in the living room.

RIGHT

*A pair of gilded baroque candlesticks illuminate
a corner of the dining room, throwing light on a
drawing by Mimmo Paladino. The artist executed
the work for von Fürstenberg on a sheet of paper
Bucarelli brought back from China, where he was
overseeing Paladino's exhibition.*

OPPOSITE

*The dining room is secluded from the entrance
by a curved sliding panel which echoes the lines
of the oval dining table and round-backed chairs.*

A VIEW OF HISTORY

ROME'S FOUNDATIONS RUN DEEP. It is not unusual to delve down into the cellar of an ancient palace only to discover stones worn smooth by carriage wheels that ran along Roman streets two thousand years ago. Many of these 'cornerstones' remain hidden beneath centuries of silt and rubble. An exception is the nineteenth-century palace that rises from the ruins of Trajan's market, its foundations perched upon what was once a row of shops along the Roman Forum.

The relatively modern apartment building dates from 1840, and was one of the first in Rome to be built under Napoleon III by a French architect. In addition to bringing northern aesthetics into play, the architect also employed up-to-the-minute technical innovations. In fact, this was one of the first buildings in Rome to use iron as a building material, and the original cast-iron shutters, bearing the stamp 'Fonderia Imperiale', remain in place to block the harsh sun.

The once grand apartments have now been divided into more manageable sizes for today's inhabitants, which include businesses as well as private residents. The apartment on these pages originally occupied the entire top floor of the building and included several grand reception rooms and boudoirs, as well as smaller service rooms at the rear, with one communal kitchen on the ground floor servicing the whole building. The top level is now split among the descendants of the original owners, who have added modern kitchens and bathrooms, and carved the larger rooms into smaller living areas to render each home independent. Yet the spaces, with their soaring ceilings and neoclassical detailing, still retain the aura of past elegance.

OPPOSITE, LEFT, AND ABOVE

*Blood-red panelling provides a suitably rich
backdrop for the owner's lavish taste in
furnishings. Many of the pieces are valuable
family heirlooms, including a pair of Louis XVI
consoles, a set of landscape panels from the
1840s by Gaspard Dughet, and blue porcelain
and bronze Sèvres vases.*

OVERLEAF

*The grand living room with its polished parquetry
floors, crimson walls and gold cornice detailing
is made functional with several velvet sofas
in streamlined shapes and plain colours.*

RIGHT

The dining room is located in a section of the apartment that was probably added onto the palace after its construction. The owner takes advantage of the high ceilings and ample wall space of this room to display his large collection of eighteenth-century Compagnie des Indes china.

OPPOSITE

The library, with its spiral staircase and loft-like gallery level, appears deceptively modern. In fact the plan of the room is original and dates to 1840.

CLASSICAL SPIRIT

WITH WALLS LINED FROM FLOOR TO CEILING WITH BOOKS, and framed prints and drawings arranged on shelves and spilling over onto the floor, it is hard to imagine a more perfect backdrop for the home of a paper restorer. Perched high above the Piazza Santa Maria in Trastevere, the apartment is a cosy warren of book-filled rooms and corridors reflecting the owner's twin passions, literature and restoration work.

Her career began with an apprenticeship to an artisan on Via Giulia, across the river. Located in one of Rome's main antique districts, this is where the owner first began her passionate collecting not only of books, but the other beautiful objects that decorate her home. Her immense collection of antique crystal reflects the sun that pours in through the large, ceiling-height windows, while her favourite blue and white Chinese porcelain pieces are grouped on all available surfaces.

More than these decorative pieces, though, it is the expansive library that wraps itself around the apartment which lends a sense of warmth and history to the environment. The rooms are literally overflowing with books. Shelves bend under their weight and piles on the floor form impromptu bases for the objects the owner picks up on her travels. Although her specialty is paper, she is fascinated by roughly sculpted wood and stone, and has brought many naively formed pieces back from her travels in India and Africa.

The furnishings are also a mix of disparate influences. Most of the pieces were inherited from her parents. Her mother, a writer, came from Sicily, while her father was Tuscan. Here, in Trastevere, north and south are brought together to form a unique setting for an ever-growing collection.

RIGHT AND OPPOSITE

*Drawings prop up books, and are in turn propped
up by sculpture. While many of the drawings
and paintings were inherited from the owner's
parents, the sculpture includes ethnographic pieces
as well as contemporary works, like the polished
wooden eggs which were crafted by a friend.*

OPPOSITE, LEFT, AND BELOW

The dining room contains much of the owner's collection of decorative objects. Antique crystal perfume bottles are displayed on a silk-covered side table, and blue and white Chinese porcelain is grouped on a round table in one corner. Among the artworks covering the walls are a delicate tapestry, an antique folding screen, and several gilt-framed paintings of classical landscapes.

ART DECO JEWEL

A BUILDING DATING FROM THE LATE 1930S is positively modern compared with the ancient architectural legacy evident everywhere in Rome. Yet for Gianni and Nicole Bulgari it proved the perfect match for a long obsession with all things art deco. Before their decorative ideas were put into place, however, the couple undertook a drastic rearrangement of the internal plan, an operation that lasted over four years

The first step was to to create a large and airy living space from what had been a series of small rooms when the apartment was owned by actress Audrey Hepburn. The exterior walls onto the terrace were then replaced by a series of sliding glass doors, left open most of the year. To unify the terrace and living room, the couple decided on a novel solution for the flooring, a pigmented resinous cement, tinted a warm egg-yolk yellow.

Much of the interior was inspired by Nicole's collection of art deco furniture, particularly English pieces from the 1930s and '40s. Many of these were acquired when she lived in London and continually bought and sold objects that took her fancy. The apartment also showcases several important bronzes from the era.

Since the couple love to entertain, they originated specific elements to meet their needs. Gianni designed the circular dining table and matching buffet, while Nicole designed the coffee table in the living room. The spacious kitchen wing, where the family spends most of its time, is divided into two connecting spaces, one for cooking, the other for informal family gatherings. Once again the whole scheme takes its cue from the 1930s, in this case a magnificent marble sink.

OPPOSITE

A unique floor treatment, yellow-tinted resinous cement, flows from the living room out onto a terrace, unifying the two spaces and creating a light-filled nest perched among the trees.

LEFT

Gianni Bulgari designed the round dining table, which is surrounded by a suite of art deco chairs. The painting of the Colosseum behind dates from the 1950s, and was one of three views of Rome found by Nicole in a London antique shop.

RIGHT

Another surprise find from Nicole's collection of 1930s furnishings, a large white cocktail cabinet with corrugated facade takes pride of place in the master bedroom. Its bold presence is more than enough to offset the lofty ceilings.

OPPOSITE

More a suite than simply a room for sleeping, the master bedroom boasts a gallery level with streamlined, art deco-style railing, reached by a sweeping stairway. Reminiscent of a Hollywood movie set, the bedroom creates a special brand of '30s glamour with its scale and sense of luxury, along with details like the palms, collection of perfume bottles, and enormous bed.

ROMAN RESTRAINT

PIAZZA VITTORIA IS UNIQUE IN ROME, as it is the city's only colonnaded piazza. Laid out under the eye of the famous northern Italian architect Gaetano Koch, the palaces that line the square mimic the classic porticoes of Torino. Built at the end of the nineteenth century to house the northern bureaucrats who came to help run the newly declared capital, these grand structures offer high ceilings, large rooms and French windows. It was these generous proportions that attracted interior designer Massimo Zompa to a dilapidated apartment in one of the palaces overlooking the piazza.

The building itself conveys a sense of down-at-heel grandeur, with its dark, winding staircase and faded paintwork, which makes stepping into Zompa's apartment all the more surprising. Pristine and warmly inviting, the interior bears the designer's trademark restrained elegance.

Zompa, who designed Karl Lagerfeld's apartment in Rome as well as Valentino's office suite, is known for his highly eclectic style of decorating, and his own completely renovated home has become a rich tapestry of patterns, textures and styles. In fact he has created several distinct areas, each with its own visual language.

The living room was constructed by knocking down a central wall to create one large room overlooking the busy piazza below. Since this is the most public of the rooms and has the most contact with life in the piazza, Zompa decided to convey a sense of the outside through the use of a wall treatment that mimicked the exterior stone blocks of the palace. The modelled plaster expanses were painted a sparkling white to create a play of shadow and light as the sun moves during the day.

ABOVE AND RIGHT

Zompa designed the fireplace and bookcases to fit within the heavily modelled panelling that defines the character of the living room. The illusion is of a single purpose-built module that wraps around the entire room. His disdain for using one single stylistic period to dictate the interior décor is amply demonstrated by the mixture of furnishings and art. The vases on top of the bookcase, for example, were designed by Zompa after details from Piranesi prints.

OPPOSITE, LEFT, AND ABOVE

The bathroom and bedroom take on an altogether softer look than the rest of the apartment. Tiles chosen for the master bathroom perfectly pick out the leaf green in the Thorpe fabric that lines the walls of the adjacent bedroom. The hexagonal marble tile, while new, echoes a typical treatment found in buildings of this period. In the bedroom, the use of the classic Thorpe print tempers the starkness of the soaring white ceiling.

A PASSIONATE AFFAIR

OLIMPIA ORSINI HAS A PASSION FOR LIFE that has infused every corner of her inspired living space. The environments she creates within each room of her two-level apartment are constantly evolving, and one special object can affect the scheme of a whole room. But it is precisely the eclectic nature of Orsini's home that makes the visitor want to move in and explore all its hidden treasures.

What intrigued Orsini most about the top two levels of the Roman palace she acquired for her home was the possibility of creating several distinct environments. Downstairs the living and dining rooms with their soaring ceilings are comfortable but classic in feeling. Upstairs Orsini let her imagination run to the romantic to create more intimate spaces.

In decorating her home Olimpia Orsini took inspiration from the palace itself, constructed upon papal commission in 1778. She has chosen mostly Louis XVI and Napoleon II furnishings, but has not followed a simple formula. There are objects from different periods and different parts of the world carefully placed throughout the apartment. Nineteenth-century American lamps from makers Pierpont and Handel sit atop seventeenth-century Italian tables; simple white broadcloth brushes against the richest silk taffetas; and humble earthenware vases stand on eighteenth-century Aubusson rugs.

Adding to the textural tapestry of the apartment is the fact that Orsini refuses to restore anything. She prefers objects to enter her home proudly wearing their history. The slightly worn quality of many of the pieces lends the rooms a very lived-in feeling, even in the more formal areas.

ABOVE AND RIGHT

Although Olimpia Orsini refers to the skylit room located just off her terrace as 'my summer kitchen', the room is much more than that. While it contains the essentials such as sink, oven and fridge, at dinner time it is transformed into a magical, candlelit setting for intimate gatherings. Many of the objects are Louis XVI, but Orsini does not confine her interior to any specific period. A slightly worn painted garden urn props up a gilded frame, while a plaster bust of an empress is draped in ivy. Any flat surface will do for the constantly changing tableaux Orsini creates with her collection of objets trouvés.

LEFT

Orsini's beloved objects even find their way into her bathroom, where impromptu still lifes include crystal candelabra, antique hand linens, and even a pair of evening shoes. The overall mood is one of femininity, with romantic nineteenth-century prints adorning the walls and a delicately sculpted eighteenth-century bust dominating the scene.

RIGHT

A nineteenth-century polychrome porcelain Bacchae holds sway over the Orangerie. A pair of eighteenth-century painted doors is propped behind, echoing the floral themes of the room.

BELOW RIGHT

A pair of nineteenth-century cast-iron vases and an antique bird cage fit perfectly in the garden-like atmosphere of the Orangerie.

OPPOSITE

High ceilings define the downstairs level, where the more formal rooms are used for entertaining guests. The salon, with its subtle gradations of ivory and antique white, has a fresh yet classic look, providing the ideal backdrop for Orsini's art and antiques. The painting is by Caucagné and dates from the end of the nineteenth century.

ABOVE

*The one defining element in the apartment is
a love of beautiful objects, patterns and textures,
which Orsini combines with a very eclectic
aesthetic. This sensibility is clearly expressed
in the bedroom, in which a wine-red check by
Valentino is paired with a classic* toile de Jouy.

OPPOSITE

*A sitting area in her husband's study displays
Orsini's passion for American folk portraits. Part
of her extensive collection of American antique
lamps is also evident here. The mix of strong
colours and unusual objects, including an antique
horn table, creates an enervating workroom.*

III.

VILLAS & PALAZZOS

NEOCLASSICAL ESTATE

PRINCE HEINRICH VON HESSEN PREFERS to use his Italian name: Principe Enrico d'Assia. It is perhaps this fact more than any other that reveals the Prince's devotion to the Villa Polissena where he now lives. The villa is a relative newcomer to Rome. In 1925 the building was a nameless farmhouse located on the estate of Villa Savoia, home to Italy's reigning royal family. When Prince Enrico's mother, the Princess Mafalda, married Prince Philip von Hessen, her father, King Victor Emmanuel III, presented them with the simple farmhouse and adjoining property as a wedding gift.

Prince Philip set about at once transforming the plain structure into an elegant neoclassical villa. Often executing the decorative work himself, he created a magical environment for his wife and two young sons. During one of his frequent trips to the local antique dealers, Prince Philip came across an eighteenth-century plaster cast of a relief portraying a queen of the house of Savoy who had also been a princess of Hesse. The prince took this as a good omen and decided to name the villa after her: Polissena.

The new owner of the estate turned his full attention to each and every room, executing a restoration so delicate, it is hard not to imagine that the villa dates from the eighteenth century. Prince Enrico has maintained the main elements of the design, preserving it as a monument to both his mother's memory and his father's exquisite taste, while making his own mark on the villa. In this idyllic setting, within the heart of Rome, Prince Enrico, who is both an artist and a stage set designer, retreats into his drawing-lined study. Within the villa, he finds the inspiration and peace to execute the fantastic watercolours for which he is known.

ABOVE, RIGHT, AND OPPOSITE

The villa's neoclassical façade, transformed by Prince Philip in the 1920s, gives little indication that the structure started out as a humble farmhouse. Nor do the gardens, now manicured and punctuated with marble statuary, even remotely echo their previous life as a grazing ground for sheep.

ABOVE AND RIGHT

*Long allées lined with hedges and cypress lead from one section of the garden
to the next. The tranquility of this setting is enhanced by the splash of formal
fountains and the singing of birds. Only the muted sound of traffic indicates
that bustling Rome lies on the other side of the tall hedge surrounding the estate.*

RIGHT AND OPPOSITE

The walls of one small bedroom are covered in handpainted eighteenth-century papers depicting Chinese scenes. As there was only so much of the precious wallpaper, one corner of the room remained blank until Prince Enrico took up his artist's brushes and filled in the missing patch.

OPPOSITE, LEFT, AND BELOW

Prince Philip's diverse collection of paintings, drawing and statuary, acquired over more than fifty years, still define the villa's interiors.

OPPOSITE

The ground floor sitting room is paved with an ancient mosaic excavated from the royal hunting grounds at Castel Porziano. However, much of this priceless floor covering is now protected by carpet. The walls and ceiling are a melange of eighteenth-century Piedmontese stucco work and fragments of painted panels depicting heavenly scenes.

LEFT

In contrast to the rococo drama of the main living room, the salon is an elegant statement in warm shades of cream, jade green and gold.

ROCOCO RETREAT

WHEN MUSSOLINI ATTEMPTED to pull Rome into the modern age during the 1930s, many of the villas, hunting lodges and pleasure pavilions dotting the perimeter of the city walls were demolished to make way for a new road network. Villa Gangalandi escaped due solely to the exquisite frescoes that cover almost every available interior surface. The villa was constructed between 1700 and 1730 by a noble Tuscan family, who hired some of the most talented artists of the day to decorate the entire building.

The frescoes in the grand, ground floor salon follow the eighteenth-century fashion for depicting recently discovered archeological finds. In fact, the documented discovery of the centaur means they can be dated to within a decade, between 1720 and 1730. Marvellous frescoes continue up to the next floor where bucolic landscapes are framed by twisted gilt columns. Even the less public rooms are patterned with foliage and exotic flowers. Many of the original eighteenth-century furnishings survive, including ingenious little sofas which open out into beds for mid-afternoon siestas. A suite of six delicate chairs in the music room still bear the blue and gilt decoration of the surrounding doors and woodwork, while an antique harpsichord is testament to the villa's original use as a place of play and relaxation.

Today's owner, who inherited the villa from her family, admits that the house lay abandoned for thirty years. Lack of electricity and plumbing made it a nice place to visit, but a difficult place to set up home. With very little aesthetic intervention, however, she has transformed this antiquated artifact into a warmly elegant environment, practical enough for modern living, yet a perfectly preserved step back into eighteenth-century Rome.

RIGHT AND OPPOSITE

In the ground floor salon, the pastoral backdrops in the wall frescoes are echoed in the sofa and armchair with their upholstery of dainty floral sprigs. The frescoes themselves, painted between 1700 and 1730, depict Minerva and a centaur in an idyllic rural setting. The artist is thought to be either Antonio Locatelli or Paolo Anesi, prominent painters of the day.

RIGHT

The second floor of the villa retains all of its original decoration. In the bedroom, the repeated floral motif on the walls and the meticulously coloured ceiling beams are handpainted. Fittingly, the furnishings have been restricted to a white bed and gilt sofa with white upholstery.

OPPOSITE, LEFT, AND BELOW

The owners have kept modern interventions to a minimum in order to preserve the villa's integrity. In the bathroom, the sink has been located centrally to avoid damaging the fresco-lined walls, while elsewhere in the house the objects displayed fit perfectly into their surroundings, from the Roman statuary, unearthed from the ancient catacombs below the villa, to the shelves lined with antique books.

A NOBLE INHERITANCE

ONCE A FOCAL POINT OF sixteenth- and seventeenth-century aristocratic life, the intersection known as the Quattro Fontane, or Four Fountains, is still one of the most dramatic sights in Rome. Four grand palaces stand on the corners of the crossroads, each marked by a fountain portraying, respectively, Strength, Fidelity, the Tiber and the Arno rivers. Rising from behind the Arno fountain stands one of the first palaces to be built at this site, now the residence of Princess Domietta Ercolani del Drago.

The palace was commissioned by Muzio Mattei in 1587, but its present incarnation dates from the beginning of the eighteenth century when the architect Alessandro Specchi added a soaring belvedere to afford sweeping views of the city. The interior, too, was reworked, and the marble paving in the entrance and stairwells dates from this time. Niches were constructed to better display owner Alessandro Albani's vast collection of antiquities, and Albani's coat of arms still decorates the frescoes and paving.

In the middle of the last century the building was acquired by Maria Cristina, the widow of Ferdinand VII of Spain, who built a grand ballroom in the garden. The del Drago family, who have lived in Rome since the fifteenth century, inherited the palace from the the widow upon her death. Princess del Drago now lives on the top floor, which incorporates the belvedere. Although she inherited most of the furnishings, and many of the paintings are family portraits, she also carries on the family tradition as an active patron of the arts. Masterpieces by some of the best-known contemporary Italian artists are a major part of her collection, and form the backdrop to her elegant abode.

ABOVE AND RIGHT

In contrast to the grand entrance hall and exterior of the palace, the living quarters of the Princess's apartment are more low-key. The large living area is filled with simple, relaxed furnishings that create several distinct areas within the one space. Interspersed among the family heirlooms are contemporary Italian works from the Princess's collection.

OPPOSITE

Unlike the rest of the apartment with its stark white walls, the formal dining room is sheathed in a patterned silk brocade, and is lit by an eighteenth-century Venetian chandelier.

LEFT

The hallway, which runs the length of the apartment, serves as a gallery for family heirlooms.

ABOVE, RIGHT, AND OPPOSITE

*The decoration of the hallways in the vast palace
probably dates from the eighteenth century when
Alessandro Albani commissioned Alessandro
Specchi to rework the interiors. Changes included
the creation of niches for displaying statuary,
and marble paving incorporating Albani's coat
of arms with its hills and stars. The massive
lion at one end of the corridor is carved from
a single block of porphyry.*

GILDED SPLENDOUR

OPPOSITE AND ABOVE
*The dining room was restored to its
original splendour by interior designer Renzo
Mongiardino. He used seventeenth- and eighteenth-
century furnishings, such as the console with
gilt-framed mirror and a neoclassical vase of*
marmo africano, *to reflect the villa's grandeur.*

THE PASTORAL BEGINNINGS OF the Casina di Grotta Pallotta date to the sixteenth century, when it was constructed as a pleasure lodge for the nearby Villa Borghese. Although the building is located today on one of Rome's busiest thoroughfares, the Via Pinciana, it was originally located amid fields and meadows. Despite having been altered over the centuries, the original design of the facade is still evident and retains the rusticated central doorway, a typical mannerist architectural conceit.

The first recorded owner was Giovanni Battista Pallotta, the nephew of a famous and powerful cardinal. Although no sign of this prestigious resident survives — no coat of arms for instance — the villa still bears his name. The most enduring legacy of any of the owners was left by Marchese Filippo de' Rossi, a Roman aristocrat, who carried out the villa's grandest decorative scheme in the mid-1700s. It was under his patronage that the grand salon was decorated, its walls treated with an illusionistic colonnade which extends the length of this already large room. The same painter also executed the small antechamber leading to the salon, incorporating scenes from *Alexander and Roxanne* and *Alexander and Diogene*.

In more recent times, the Count and Countess Aldo Brachetti Peretti have made their mark on the villa, carefully restoring the magnificent frescoes to their original brilliance. They entrusted the interior of the villa to decorator Renzo Mongiardino, who respected the style and period elements of the original designs. The only change made to the garden was to substitute the eighteenth-century fountain with a swimming pool that retains the fountain's original shape.

LEFT AND BELOW

A ground floor suite of rooms was recently renovated by interior designer Toni Facella to form an apartment for the owner's son. The main salon retains its original stucco work and is dominated by towering French doors and a large eighteenth-century painting by Andriessen.

RIGHT AND OPPOSITE

*The grand salon was decorated in the eighteenth-
century with a mural depicting an illusionistic
colonnade. A pair of seventeenth-century
candelabra flanking the fireplace were designed
by Borromini, while a modern sculpture by Henry
Moore takes pride of place. The central door of
the expansive room is surmounted by a cameo-like
bust of Homer, whose detailed features may reflect
those of the original eighteenth-century patron.*

125

RENAISSANCE CITADEL

The main hall on the castle's second floor boasts an original paved floor – complete with bumps and uneven bricks – and intricate beamed ceiling. Mounted above the mantelpiece of the enormous fireplace is a carved wooden plaque bearing the Orsini coat of arms. Ancestral portraits of the Marescottis line the walls.

TO UNDERSTAND THE ARCHITECTURAL HISTORY of Vignanello, just north of Rome, it helps to know the Ruspoli family's eventful past. Vignanello began life in the ninth century as a Benedictine monastery but was reinvented as a military fortress, passing from one noble family to the next until 1531, when Pope Paolo III gave the castle to his niece, Ortensia Baglioni, and her husband, a courtier named Marescotti, part of the Ruspoli family.

The couple immediately called in Renaissance architect Antonio da Sangallo, who transformed the rough fortress into a comfortable villa where the couple took up residence. The garden was built during the next generation by Ortensia's nephew, Marcantonio Marescotti, and his wife Ottavia.

The rather sober interiors of this fortress-turned-villa took shape in the eighteenth century under Francesco Maria Ruspoli. An astute businessman, Ruspoli funded the restoration of the castle at Vignanello and acquired the great family palace in central Rome. He was an active patron of the arts, and often invited his friend Handel to his country estate. It was here that the composer wrote parts of the *Resurrection*, dedicated to his benefactor.

Today Vignanello is the responsibility of the Princesses Claudia and Giada Ruspoli, who inherited it from their father, Prince Sforza Ruspoli. Slowly, Claudia and her sister are attempting to restore the palace — frayed over the centuries — to its former splendour. The secret garden, nestled below the ramparts on a lower level, is being replanted and remodelled to reflect its original design. An entire network of grottoes and caves is being cleared out, revealing a magical labyrinth of underground passages that stretch for miles — just one of many layers of family history now being uncovered.

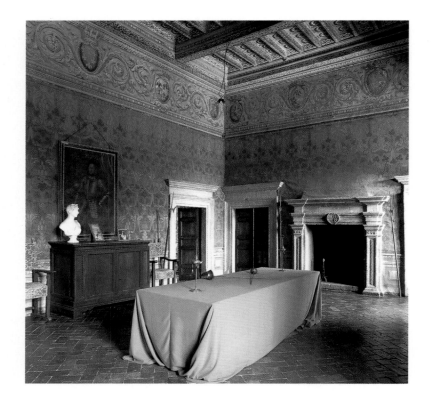

ABOVE

This grand hall served most recently as the dining room of Princess Claudia Ruspoli's grandparents. The carved mantelpiece still bears the coat of arms, which was partially effaced in the sixteenth century after Ortensia Baglioni killed her husband, a Marescotti.

RIGHT

The garden is one of the finest examples of a box parterre in Italy, initially laid out in fragrant rosemary and sage. The box hedges retain the original design incorporating the linked initials of Ottavia Orsini, whose father designed the nearby garden at Bomarzo, and her sons Sforza and Galeazzo.

OPPOSITE AND LEFT

Displayed at the entrance to the main salon are ancient halberds from the family's arms collection. Inside the salon, the brocade covered walls are topped by a frieze with the family coat of arms.

BELOW

The private chapel is dedicated to the family's patron saint, Giacinta Marescotti. Her brown habit is enshrined near the altar.

RIGHT AND OPPOSITE

*The castle's origins as a fortress are recalled
in the main entrance hall, which opens onto
the town square, and in the drawbridge leading
to the garden. Military troops would have once
clattered over the original stone and brick
paving on their way in and out of the citadel.
Today, antique weapons are displayed under
the vaulted ceilings.*

OPPOSITE AND LEFT

The decoration of the bedrooms dates to the first decades of this century when Princess Ruspoli's grandparents made this their primary home. These days the rooms remain empty most of the year, until the entire family descends on Vignanello during the summer months.

IV.

COLLECTORS' HOMES

TIFFANY MAGIC

IT COMES AS NO SURPRISE that this exceedingly dramatic apartment perched high above Piazza del Popolo was conceived by a film director and set designer. Together, Lina Wertmuller and Enrico Job have created a fantasy world where mirrors reflect rich, dark velvets, art nouveau glass and mysterious paintings.

When the couple first came across the apartment in 1970, it had been on the market for quite some time, rejected by others due to its small size and rather awkward layout. Not deterred in the least, Wertmuller was captivated by the magnificent views from the rooftop terrace, and had complete confidence that her husband could work his magic.

After three years of gutting and reconstruction their new home was ready to house a quirky collection of art nouveau lamps and furnishings. To create a sense of unity Job chose wood panelling to accentuate the flow from one room to another. While the apartment is on the top floor, and has breathtaking views, all of the main windows are located along one wall of the deep living room. To extend the space, as well as reflect the available light, Job installed large banks of mirrors along the interior walls.

Before embarking on a career in set design in 1973, Job was an artist, so many of the artworks and furnishings, including the coffee table, are by him. A particularly lucky discovery was the ceiling decoration that now adorns the living room. While on the lookout for a landscape backdrop for a film he was working on, Job came across this turn-of-the-century canvas in a warehouse. Miraculously it fit perfectly, both physically and aesthetically, into the ceiling of their newly created living room.

ABOVE

Echoing the colours and decorative devices of the living room, the dining area features wood panelling to create a sense of warmth. To prevent the room looking too heavy, a large mirror above the fireplace is used to reflect the light outside. A fire is lit in the grate on most winter evenings.

OPPOSITE

A large portrait of the Countess Mattei presides over one corner of the living room, complementing the rich colours of the interior. The countess was most famously the lover of the turn-of-the-century poet, writer, artist and politician Gabriele D'Annunzio, notorious for his decadent lifestyle.

OPPOSITE AND LEFT

Floral and botanical themes run throughout the apartment, from the rich velvet brocades with their bunches of vivid flowers draped over the couches, to the delicate motifs on the ceiling panel, the vases full of dried flowers, and the designs of the art nouveau lamps themselves.

MUSEUM PIECES

Giorgio Franchetti's study holds his most prized possession: his sizable collection of art. As there are far too many paintings to be displayed on the walls of the house at the one time, Franchetti regularly rotates them. When not on show, they are stored on open shelving, allowing Franchetti to easily pull out large canvases, such as these two by Tano Festa, for contemplation and study.

WHEN GIORGIO AND GAIA FRANCHETTI bought an abandoned candle factory as the site for their new home, its restoration seemed a daunting prospect. Yet amid the rubble, broken windows and old wax moulds, Giorgio Franchetti sensed the presence of something grander. Sure enough, as reconstruction work began, the remains of an old Roman house were uncovered, complete with mosaic pavement fragments. Franchetti's ancient Roman aesthetic for restoring the house now had a historical underpinning.

The house is made up of three wings which wrap themselves around a central courtyard. The tall glazed windows respect the building's industrial past, while the marble columns supporting the portico give the feeling of an ancient Roman impluvium. In fact the whole plan of the house, which is inward looking and blind to the street, reflects the ancient Roman distribution of space. The central courtyard, open to the elements, was a central feature of all Roman houses. In this modern rendition a fountain and a symmetrically planted vegetable garden are the central decorative elements.

Inside, the house has become a gallery of sorts, its walls hung with the vivid modern artworks Giorgio collects, several Cy Twombly pieces among them. The emphasis on colour extends to the furnishings, the result of Gaia's long love affair with things Indian. Many of the fabrics are from her textile collection, which combines hand-loomed Indian fabric with antique Roman and Indian designs. Although the Indian-influenced interior was originally unintentional, the restoration of the house highlighted the affinities between the Indian and Roman cultures. Both, Gaia realized, were based on a similar sense of classicism and made ideal partners.

ABOVE, RIGHT, AND OPPOSITE

When the Franchettis first bought the property,
the courtyard was a tangled mess of machinery,
vats and old wax moulds from the candle factory.
They have transformed it into a tranquil oasis,
complete with vegetable garden and fish pond.

RIGHT AND OPPOSITE

*Every spare inch of wall space, whether in an
alcove in the hallway or Gaia Franchetti's design
studio, is used for the exhibition of the couple's
collection of modern art. In Gaia's studio the
paintings jostle for room with piles of the hand-
loomed Indian fabrics she creates for her line
of curtains, bedspreads, table cloths and towels.
The fabric patterns invariably incorporate antique
Roman and Indian designs.*

OPPOSITE

*Modern and antique elements co-exist happily
in the living room. The pale yellow walls echo
the gilding on the panelled doors, while providing
a neutral backdrop for the paintings of Tano Festa,
an artist Giorgio Franchetti considers a genius.*

LEFT

*A skylight was opened in the stairwell to light this
passage hung with modern paintings. The panelled
doors with scrolled surround are a reminder of
Rome's much older artistic heritage.*

151

ANCIENT OBSESSION

PERCHED AMID THE DOMES OF RENAISSANCE CHURCHES, a stone's throw from the Vatican, Federico Forquet's apartment reads like a richly illustrated volume of antique history, and is in every minute detail a reflection of its creator. Classic aptly describes Forquet's style, but not the cool detached neo-classicism of preceding centuries — his version is a modern revisitation of the traditional through the warm tones of the Mediterranean.

The first floor of the apartment is the most formal, since this is where the salon and dining room are located. Handpainted canvases, designed by Forquet, cover the walls and wrap the living room in a rich pattern of trompe l'oeil columns and framed vases. Elsewhere in the room vases on pedestals echo the motif, inspired by a number of fifth-century Greek urns Forquet inherited from his grandfather.

Another recurring theme is Forquet's home town of Naples. Views of the southern city appear almost everywhere. A powerful scene of Vesuvius erupting adds to the dramatic feeling of the salon, while more tranquil views of the bay are displayed in the private upstairs sitting room.

The sitting room, which opens off the bedroom, is a peaceful light-filled retreat from the busy streets below. Glowing tones and soft cotton curtains floating in the breeze lend a pastoral feeling to this captivating space and add warmth to a room dominated by antiquities. On a side table Forquet keeps his most precious possessions: a large collection of mosaic miniatures, portraying landscapes, monuments and celebrated views. His love for ancient stones is evident in the porphyry decorating the mantelpiece, which provides the focus of the sitting area.

RIGHT AND OPPOSITE

A small attic space tucked beneath the oak-beamed roof is reached by a staircase leading up from the sitting room. Decorated in soft gold tones, this is Forquet's private study, where he works on designs for interiors and fabrics. He surrounds himself with favourite objects to fire his creativity, including prized pieces from his extensive collection of miniature monuments, marble ornaments and ancient stone fragments.

ABOVE AND OPPOSITE

Layers of rich russet and bronze create a striking environment for the
formal living room. An Empire console is flanked by a pair of candelabra
by F. Righetti. The room is dominated by Chevalier Volaire's large
eighteenth-century painting depicting the eruption of Vesuvius.

OPPOSITE AND LEFT
Forquet carefully positioned his bed to take
full advantage of the magnificent view of Rome's
domed churches from his window. An eighteenth-
century writing desk with an embossed leather lid
is used to display a group of miniature paintings.

A MODERN FIXATION

OVER THE PAST DOZEN YEARS Douglas Andrews has lived a rather itinerant life in the Eternal City, constantly searching for dilapidated apartments, fixing them up, and moving on to the next challenge. His most recent apartment, originally a rabbit warren of cramped dark rooms, presented a whole new set of problems to solve. It was not the ideal environment to showcase Andrews' prized collection of modern paintings, but the eighteenth-century terra-cotta floors convinced him that the apartment could work.

One of the first tasks was to knock down half the internal walls, creating five light and airy rooms from the original ten. The expansive white walls and warm, textured floor serve as an ideal backdrop for the art collection. Even the furnishings having been carefully chosen not to detract from the paintings. They are functional yet also somewhat anonymous.

For the dining room, Andrews fashioned a long white oval table from a bare wooden board, which he painted with white undercoat and sealed with a layer of wax to lend an almost translucent appearance. In the living room, originally four separate rooms, two large, comfortable white sofas are perfect for entertaining yet offer no visual distractions from the paintings.

Another crucial problem to solve was how to light the rooms. Andrews did not want to clutter them with lamps, which produce a flattering light for people but not for viewing paintings. At the same time, he wanted to avoid the look of a professional gallery. Instead of typical track lighting, small halogen lamps were recessed into niches carved out in the ceiling. The resulting light, while lending focus to an ever-changing display of artworks, is diffuse enough to create a warm and luminous ambience.

BELOW, RIGHT, AND OPPOSITE

The living room contains an ever-changing collection of paintings, drawings and sculpture. A small work by abstract expressionist Franz Kline is displayed on an easel atop a rustic table. Dating from 1952, it is one of the earliest pieces in Andrews' collection. Other works include Luigi Ontani's totemic ceramic sculpture with gleaming metallic bust, which stands before a large monochromatic canvas by Donald Baechler.

OPPOSITE AND LEFT

*Andrews found the eighteenth-century wrought-iron canopy bed in a Rome antique shop and immediately acquired it for his guest room.
To one side of the bed an entire wall of the guest room is given over to shelves housing Andrews' collection of exhibition catalogues and art books.*

ANTIQUARIAN ASSETS

ALTHOUGH ROME HAS GROWN into a major European capital over the last few decades, much of its infrastructure has yet to catch up with its rapid growth. The roads that lead into the city, for example, remain the antique roads of Rome: the Appia, the Cassia and the Salaria. Along one such byway, art historian Federico Zeri built his country retreat twenty years ago.

When Zeri first chose this area, only a short drive from Rome's centre, the rolling hills were disturbed only by the seasonal plough that tilled the fields. While land development has encroached upon his idyllic views, his own well-tended fruit orchard, olives groves and rose gardens recall those of the villas of Seneca and Agrippa, which were once located here.

For the last two decades Zeri has made this country estate his home. Apart from the obvious attractions of the garden and orchard, the main reason for abandoning Rome's busy centre was to find space for his collection of books. Numbering some 80,000 volumes, Zeri's library, specializing in art history, rivals that of some of the best public libraries in the country. Paired with his extensive photographic archive of over 100,000 photos documenting works of art, it is a vast resource for his ongoing research.

Like scholars of old, Zeri has filled his library with artworks as well. Tapestries and paintings adorn the walls, while sculpture ranging from Roman times to baroque seems to cover every available level surface, and great chunks of ancient porphyry are piled in corners. Zeri's particular passion is Roman inscriptions and here the house itself is not large enough to contain his collection. The walls surrounding his garden are encrusted with these ancient fragments, which bear testament to Roman events long past.

ABOVE AND RIGHT

*A rococo mix of colours, styles and patterns, the living room reveals the scope
of Zeri's enthusiastic collecting. Baroque marble busts of cardinals and swirling
bronze figures compete for space with seventeenth-century oil paintings and
an enormous seventeenth-century tapestry in gold and blue covering one wall.*

RIGHT AND OPPOSITE

Zeri's vast library of books spills over from the shelves to the floor. The library numbers over 80,000 volumes, rivalling the collections of many private institutions, and enables the scholar to conduct most of his research at home.

Opposite

Zeri's dining room incorporates architectural elements like carved marble portals from ancient palazzos, as well as his collection of statuettes. The star of the room, however, is a magnificent long white table inlaid with green marble.

Left and Above

In the reception hall, art holds sway, creating an impressive gallery of Roman busts, inscriptions, urns and marble fragments.

ABOVE RIGHT,
RIGHT, AND OPPOSITE

*Outside, roses and lavender perfume the air
and entwine the countless ancient mosaics and
carved Roman inscriptions that Zeri displays
in the garden adjacent to the villa.*

V.

GARDEN SPACES

AN ENCHANTED GARDEN

OPPOSITE AND ABOVE
The floral theme begins indoors and moves out onto the terrace, where scented climbing roses perfume the air while also providing an element of privacy. Overlooking Rome's botanical gardens, the terrace is furnished with nineteenth-century French patio tables and chairs. Cushioned banquettes stretch invitingly under one of the garden's towering coconut palms. What appears to be a dolls' house in one corner, is in fact an unusual eighteenth-century bird house.

INTERIOR DESIGNER DIANE BURN BERTUZZI scoured Rome for a decade in search of a permanent home before she finally settled on an apartment in Rome's Trastevere neighbourhood. Although the living space was arguably too small for her husband, daughter and herself, a thousand-square-foot terrace jutting out over Rome's botanical gardens, Orto Botanica, more than compensated. Through Burn's creative talents, the rest of the apartment has been transformed to reflect the ancient Roman garden it overlooks.

Burn's trademark style, which features elaborate mural decorations and fantasy finishes, has always emphasized natural motives. Here, the apartment's location inspired Burn to carry these themes even further. The entrance sets the mood as an 'inner courtyard', festooned with painted foliage and vines, as well as a continuous supply of fresh flowers.

The garden theme continues upstairs in the salon, with its wall mural evoking an enchanted gazebo. The vibrant green tones are given depth with underlying shades of ochre and terra cotta. Here, as throughout the apartment, Burn chose sisal to cover the floors, both for its natural feel as well as the illusion it creates of the apartment nestling in a big woven basket.

Rome's climate enables the family to treat the terrace as their outdoor living and dining room six months of the year. The rest of the time, Burn holds her frequent dinner parties in an intimately scaled dining room. She has chosen to enlarge the space optically, through clever placement of a pair of eighteenth-century mirrors and a trompe l'oeil niche. At night, lit only by candles, the room shimmers and floats between the reflected light of gilt mirrors and the garden stretching out beyond the French doors.

OPPOSITE

Since Burn's interiors rely so heavily on special finishes, her relationships with the various artists who translate her ideas are crucial. For the dining room, barely big enough to fit a table, Burn wanted to create a theatrical backdrop as well as the impression of more space.

LEFT

Once a week the entry hall becomes Burn's potting studio. She returns from the markets armed with fresh flowers to fill the apartment, arranging them in an array of vases, baskets and antique French terra-cotta pots.

RIGHT AND OPPOSITE

Burn's passion is for all things French, particularly furniture dating from the eighteenth century, as is evident in the living room. Many of the antiques, such as the wood and tole columns, have followed Burn from New York to Paris to Rome.

OPPOSITE, LEFT, AND BELOW
Whether in the entry hall with its floral-themed mural, a child's bedroom with luxuriously draped lit à la polonaise, or the master bathroom, the tone of Burn's apartment is delightfully romantic.

TERRACE VIEW

ROME IS A CITY OF SURPRISES — gardens hidden behind high walls, frescoed ceilings in dilapidated fourth floor walk-ups — but by far the most interesting surprises are those that reflect the personalities and quirks of the people Rome attracts: transplanted foreigners who bring a little bit of home with them and fit it into Rome's ancient setting.

Palazzo Pico, a nineteenth-century palace overlooking the dome of Sant' Andrea della Valle, houses one such haven for an art history professor from Piedmont, Italy's most northerly province. It is this northern sensibility, attuned for comfort and the pleasure of seasonal living, that has informed his home, an apartment on the palace rooftop, complete with the modern conveniences of doorman and elevator.

The interior is neither fussy nor perfect, and is designed to provide a comfortable space where friends are always welcome. Although most of the apartment was left untouched structurally, one thing the owner insisted on was a double-faced fireplace, which opens onto both the library and salon. No northern home would be complete without it. Fireplaces, velvets and royal memorabilia create the illusion that the apartment is in Torino, Piedmont's cultured capital city and seat of the Italian monarchy.

The terrace, which is enormous and covers almost half of the building's roof, has become a sort of warm weather abode to mirror the winter apartments below. The plants, which include fragrant jasmine, rugosa roses and budelaia, artfully divide the rooftop into sitting areas and dining areas, even a tiny kitchen. Completing the picture is the elegant dome of the Sant' Andrea della Valle that looms beyond the terrace.

ABOVE AND RIGHT

*The spacious terrace has been artfully divided by shrubs and pots to form
several distinct areas, including an open-air dining room, complete with
thatched roof to provide shade, a sitting room, and even a summer kitchen.*

Right and Opposite

*The double-faced fireplace, which opens
onto the living room as well as the library, is a
typically northern Italian addition to this Roman
apartment. Most of the furniture, as well as
the carved marble mantelpiece, were brought
by the owner from his home in Piedmont.*

OPPOSITE AND LEFT

*A rich array of interior objects attests to
the ornate tastes of Italy's northern provinces.
The tulip-shaped tin lamps, originally used
for church processionals, are heirlooms from
the owner's family chapel in Piedmont. Miniature
portraits of his ancestors, and of members of the
royal family of Savoy, hang on brocade pulls.*

PLEASURE PAVILION

OPPOSITE AND ABOVE

*It is hard to believe that this wooden chalet lies
in the centre of Rome. When Suspisio first saw
the building, it had been abandoned for over forty
years and a tree was growing through the roof.
Now it provides a tranquil retreat in the midst of
a rambling garden. Outside the house, an ornately
carved Balinese bed creates a luxurious niche.*

HALFWAY UP ROME'S GIANICOLO HILL lies the green oasis that Guia
Suspisio has literally carved out for herself. The Gianicolo has provided a cool
retreat for Romans for thousands of years. Summer villas, parks and pleasure
pavilions have always dotted this verdant slope, taking advantage of the
splendid views, cooling breezes and proximity to the city centre. It is only
during the present century that urban development has begun to encroach
on the once formal gardens and fields of wild flowers.

Suspisio was lucky enough to find a small corner, untouched by time,
in which to create her own secluded retreat. The property she found was a
steeply sloping piece of land with a lovely villa, most likely a seventeenth-
century hunting lodge. A wild and abandoned garden stretched up beyond,
criss-crossed by winding paths and brick stairways.

At first Suspisio and her family intended to restore the villa to live in,
but as they began to hack their way into the overgrown back garden, using
a machete to make their way through the thick vegetation, a picturesque
wooden cottage from the turn of the nineteenth century was revealed.
It was this folly, constructed by some long forgotten pleasure seeker, that they
decided to take as their new home.

After years of work the cottage has been restored, the wild parkland
around it now tamed but still providing a protective leafy buffer. It is
a surprising slice of English country style right in the middle of Rome,
complete with a bucolic garden dotted with baroque fountains and grottoes.
The villa has also been renovated to retain its more formal atmosphere, and
is used for parties or by clients who want a share of this private paradise.

V · GARDEN SPACES

RIGHT

*For her living room, Suspisio has retained the
low proportions of the original ceiling to create
warm and intimate spaces not usually found in
Rome's more palatial interiors. The room evokes
the spirit and charm of an English country home.*

196

OPPOSITE AND LEFT

Oriental elements, including the split bamboo that lines the ceilings and a brass gong hanging on one wall, lend an exotic quality to the garden room. The full-length nude echoes the lines of the long sofas and the curved recliner, all designed to make this a room for complete relaxation.

PASTORALE

IN A CITY FULL OF ETERNAL MONUMENTS it is rare to find a house built expressly so that it will one day melt back into the landscape. Yet that is exactly why Giovanni Sanjust decided to build his home entirely out of wood. Sanjust, whose specialty is painted furniture and frescoes, chose timber instead of the typical stone or brick construction because it is clean, warm, and, above all, biodegradable. Just as importantly it is also cheap and quick to work with. As a carpenter he did most of the work himself, and the nucleus was built in less than two months. Later additions to accommodate his growing family have been accomplished in subsequent two-month stages. Almost every piece of furniture in the house has been made by Sanjust.

The property is located a short drive from Rome's centre, where Sanjust once worked from an eighteenth-century studio. His spacious new home seems even larger than its five acres, perhaps because it accommodates such a wide array of plant and animal life. The landscape is dotted with clusters of unusual trees, cultivated from seedlings collected from around the world. Two hundred chickens, in ten exotic breeds, provide eggs, while the wild boar and rare white pigs provide company. Add to this five dogs and two horses, and the menagerie is complete.

When not taking care of his brood or tending the grounds, Sanjust retreats into a tropical greenhouse where, amid towering exotic plants, he has set up his studio. While a separate workshop is reserved for practical carpentry projects, here he labours over small models for his large-scale frescoes and painting commissions, viewed in the soft dappled light that filters through a canopy of palm fronds and ferns.

ABOVE AND RIGHT

The house reveals Sanjust's twin passions. The first is bonsai, and the twisted, sculptural shapes of the trees he cultivates are rooted in terra-cotta pots around the grounds. The second obsession is rare poultry breeds, some of which can be glimpsed in the garden. Indoors, the artist includes the animals in his paintings and decorated household objects, such as the two log bins by the fireplace.

OPPOSITE

The floral motifs on the study cabinets are typical examples of the meticulous work Sanjust executes upon commission. When he paints large-scale murals for clients he likes to keep the original, smaller sketch to hang in his own home.

LEFT

Produce from the family's large vegetable garden makes the household almost self-sufficient, and also brings bold splashes of colour to the kitchen.

LIVING IN ROME

Rome is home to some of the world's best-known, and loved, monuments: the Colosseum, St. Peter's Basilica, and Bernini's fountains in Piazza Navona. But one of Rome's charms is that for all its magnificence, pomp, and sense of history, it remains a city on a human scale. Although several residential neighbourhoods pool out beyond the core, Rome's heart is easily crossed by foot. In fact the *passeggiata*, or stroll, is a way to see, be seen and get through the day's activities. Any visitor to Rome immediately notes the casual elegance of its strolling inhabitants. They have a sense of style that is entirely in keeping with the classic tenor of the city.

Conveniently, the most popular clothing stores are located within easy walking distance of one another, along the streets radiating from the Piazza di Spagna, at the bottom of the Spanish Steps. Via Condotti, Via Frattina and Via Borgognona are home to most of the big names in Italian fashion: Armani, Prada, Gucci, Versace and Valentino. Gente on Via Frattina and Alexander on Piazza di Spagna offer a selection of designs from younger and foreign labels. Several stores have created lines available only in their Rome shops. Bomba on Via dell'Oca sells original designs that combine simple elegance with exquisite materials. The De Clercq sisters' store on Via delle Carozze offers a range of handmade knits in silk, cotton and linen. Ivory, brass and antique buttons make each sweater a small work of art.

As with its fashions, Rome's interiors are, by and large, less cutting-edge than those in Milan, but there are several stores that carry the most recent furniture designs. Spazio Sette, off Largo Argentina, covers three floors of a sixteenth-century palazzo, filled with everything from ashtrays to sofa beds. Ex-ante, in Largo Toniolo, is decidedly more avant-garde, with a smaller, though more original, stock of objects. For the Italian design classics, shoppers head to Forma

OPPOSITE
AND ABOVE
*Quintessential
Roman sights: the
marble statues of
Bernini's Fountain
of the Four Rivers in
Piazza Navona, and
St. Peter's Basilica
in the Vatican.*

207

Memoria in Trastevere. Still, many Romans would never think of walking into a store to buy a ready-made couch, when the city offers such a wide cross section of artisans.

The first stop is at Cesare, Rubelli or Giorgio e Febbi for lengths of heavy Italian brocades and silks. Next stop is a small upholsterer like Amedeo on Via Boschetto where the *tappezziera* can produce any object desired, from their own source books, or from a picture you bring in. For the kitchen and bath, handpainted tiles from all over Italy — both antique and modern — are for sale at Farnese in a museum-like showroom on Piazza Farnese. Finishing touches like trompe l'oeil, custom-made cabinetry and metal work are common even in the simplest apartments, and artisans' ateliers are located in the narrow streets of the old neighbourhoods. Romans devote even more energy to imbibing than shopping. They start their workday early, all the better to incorporate as many coffee breaks as possible. Besides the first quick espresso in the morning, the mid-morning break is a ritual. Caffé Greco offers a turn-of-the-century atmosphere where the likes of Shelley, Byron and Keats used to congregate. At Sant' Eustachio, just a block from the Pantheon, little cups of espresso are prepared behind a curtain, to protect a secret recipe that results in one of the smoothest cups of coffee in the city. Early on in the day, attention is turned to important dinner plans. For those who want to eat at home, but don feel like cooking, Volpetti, on Via della Scrofa, has an array of roasted meats, pastas and stuffed vegetables. For those whose passion is cooking, Campo dei Fiori is one of the most picturesque open markets in the world. Piles of artichokes, mounds of

RIGHT

The majestic sweep of the Spanish Steps leads up to the twin bell towers of the sixteenth-century Trinità dei Monti.

LEFT

The presidential palace takes its name from one of Rome's original seven hills, the Quirinale.

lemons and baskets of oranges perfume the air. One end of the piazza is dedicated to cut flowers and the other to fish. In between, vendors wheel in their carts full of fruits and vegetables, both local and exotic. The specialty stores which ring the piazza offer meat, sausages, cheese and freshly baked pizza and bread as well as handmade pasta.

Although Romans do entertain at home, they more often meet friends at a favourite restaurant. In fact, dining out is the preferred evening entertainment of most of the city's inhabitants. A perennial favourite is Nino's, a restaurant specializing in Tuscan cuisine. A constantly bubbling pot of beans in the entranceway entices weary shoppers to pause for a fragrant bowl of hearty soup for lunch. Special occasions are celebrated at Piperno's in the ghetto, two blocks from the synagogue. Large tables of families celebrating birthdays and anniversaries alternate with smaller groups of the city's elite feasting on Jewish specialties such as fried artichokes, cured meats, and 'grandfather's balls' — deep fried, chocolate-filled balls of ricotta — for dessert.

RIGHT

Caffé della Pace's cozy interior is a constant draw for the artistic and intellectual set. However, it is the tables in the piazza outside that are always most popular.

One of the more recent, and welcome, additions to Rome's eating scene has been the proliferation of wine bars. These have sprung up attached to some of the most respected wine merchants, who have set up tables amid the shelves of bottles and begun to offer from light snacks to full-fledged gourmet meals.

Santa Maria del Pianto, in the ghetto, was initiators of this trend, offering a tantalizing display appetizers, pastas and desserts. The bar's hand-made cheeses are unique in the city, and a selection is served with the house specialty, mostarda di pomodoro, an intensely concentrated confit of tomatoes.

Several restaurants present authentic 'scenes' as well as offering excellent food. Pierluigi, in Piazza de' Ricci, gets going at around ten and is where Rome's beautiful people gather for late-night meals and table-hopping in the intimate piazza. A large display of fresh fish and a groaning antipasto table guarantee a good meal along with a glamorous evening. Ar Galletto is located in one of Rome's most beautiful squares, Piazza Farnese. Although the area is closed to traffic, it's not uncommon to see a movie star pulling up in his white Jaguar convertible for a quick serving of the restaurant's famous Galletto al Diavolo, or Devil's Chicken, which is covered in cracked pepper and roasted between two heavy bricks.

Rome is known for its cucina povera, or 'poor' cuisine, which makes use of rough ingredients including organ meats, wild greens and strong cheeses. While there are still some simple trattoria that serve up these specialties, like Grappolo d'Oro on Via della Cancelleria, they are far outnumbered these days by fancier establishments using more costly ingredients. Quinzi e Gabrielli and La Rosetta have gained their deservedly high reputation by serving the freshest seafood, which arrives each evening from the nearby port of Fiumicino. La Gensola, in Trastevere, offers a simpler, Sicilian version of seafood.

Although Rome does have a club scene, the chic crowd tends to congregate at several bars near Piazza Navona. Caffé della Pace serves drinks and coffee far into the night, its crowds spilling outside to fill up the pavement tables. In nearby Piazza del Fico, named for the large fig tree growing in the square, Bar del Fico attracts artists, intellectuals and the late-night crowd, who gather here to while away their time until the small hours.

LEFT

When Rome's well-heeled residents tire of looking at their art collections, like this one which includes several Cy Twombly sculptures, they head for less cerebral pursuits at Pierluigi.

211

VISITOR'S GUIDE

Clothes

Bomba
Via dell'Oca 39
T 361 2881

De Clercq & De Clercq
Via delle Carrozze 5
T 679 0988

Dulce Vidoza
Via dell'Orso 58
T 689 3007

Gente
Via Frattina 69
T 678 9132

Fendi
Via Borgognona
38/39/40
T 679 7641

Armani
Via dei Condotti 77
T 699 1460

Prada
Via dei Condotti 92/95
T 679 0897

Gucci
Via dei Condotti 8
T 678 9340

Versace
Via Bocca di Leone 26
T 678 0521

clothes cont'd...

Valentino
Via Bocca di Leone 16
T 679 5862

Alexander
Piazza di Spagna 51
T 6994 0167

Mia Carmen
Via Panisperna
T 485 622

Josephine de Huertas
Via di Parione 19/20
T 6830 0156

Maga Morgana
Via del Governo Vecchio 27
T 687 9995

Shoes

AVC Adriana Campanile
Piazza di Spagna 88
T 678 0095

Borini
Via dei Pettinari 86
T 687 5670

Salvatore Ferragamo
Via dei Condotti 73/74
T 679 1565

Herzel
Via del Babuino 123
T 678 3384

shoes cont'd...

Sergio Rossi
Piazza di Spagna 97/100
T 678 3245

Fragiacomo
Via dei Condotti 35
T 679 8780

Restaurants

Nino's
Via Borgognona 11
T 679 5676

Fiaschetteria Beltramme
Via della Croce 39

Ristorante al 34
Via Mario de' Fiori 34
T 679 5091

L' Enoteca Antica
Via della Croce 76
T 679 0896

Piperno
Via Monte dei Cenci 9
T 6880 2772

La Gensola
Piazza della Gensola 15
T 581 6312

Ar Galletto
Piazza Farnese 102
T 686 1714

restaurants cont'd...

Pierluigi
Piazza de' Ricci 144
T 686 8717

Quinzi e Gabrielli
Via Coppelle 5
T 687 9389

La Rosetta
Via della Rosetta 8
T 686 1002

Grappolo d'Oro
Via della Cancelleria 80
T 686 4118

Pizzerias

Baffetto
Via del Governo
Vecchio 114 T 686 1617

Francesco al Fico
Piazza del Fico 29
T 686 4009

Leoncino
Via del Leoncino 28
T 687 6306

Bars

Bar Sant'Eustachio
Piazza Sant'Eustachio 82
T 686 1309

bars cont'd...

Caffé della Pace

Via della Pace 3/7

T 686 1216

Bar del Fico

Piazza del Fico 26

T 686 5205

Caffé Greco

Via dei Condotti 86

T 679 1700

Wine Bars

Bottega del Vino

Via Santa Maria

del Pianto 9

T 686 5970

Il Simposio di Piero

Costantini

Piazza Cavour 16

T 321 1502

Trimani il Wine Bar

Via Cernaia 37b

T 446 9630

Food Stores

Castroni

Via Cola di Rienzo 196

Rosticceria Volpetti

Via della Scrofa 31/32

T 686 1940

Furnishings

Forma e Memoria

Vicolo di S. Onofrio 24

T 683 2915

Cesari

Via del Babuino 195

T 361 3451

Giorgio e Febbi

Piazza Rotunda 61/62

T 679 1649

Rubelli

Via Due Macelli 80/82

T 679 5165

Spazio Sette

Via dei Barbieri 7

T 6830 7139

Art & Antiques

Main shopping streets

Via de' Coronari

Via del Babuino

Via Margutta

Christie's

Palazzo Massimo

Lancellotti

Piazza Navona 114

T 687 2787

art & antiques cont'd...

Finarte

Via Margutta 54

T 320 7638

Jewellery

Massimo Maria Melis

Via dell'Orso 57

T 686 9188

Bulgari

Via Condotti 10

T 679 3876

Diego Percossi Papi

Via di S. Eustachio 16

T 6880 1466

Elena Levi Palazzolo

Via Arco dei Tolomei 4

T 580 6745

Hotels

Carriage

Via delle Carrozze 36

T 679 3312

Del Sole al Pantheon

Piazza della Rotonda 63

T 678 0441

Hotel d'Inghilterra

Via Bocca di Leone 14

T 699 81

hotels cont'd...

Grand Hotel Plaza

Via del Corso 126

T 6992 1111

Duca D'Alba

Via Leonina 14

T 484 471

Residences

Palazzo Al Velabro

Via Velabro 16

T 679 2758

Residenza di Ripetta

Via Ripetta 231

T 322 2341

Personalized Guided Tours

Associazione Culturale

Studio Olympia

Via Belsiana 7

T 6992 0731

F 678 0942

Scooter Rental

I Bike Rome

T 322 5240/361 3307

A C K N O W L E D G M E N T S

The publishers would like to thank:
Valentino, Carlos Souza, Filippo del Drago, and all those who
graciously opened their homes to be photographed.

To my father, Joseph Helman, whose love affair with
the Eternal City inspired my own passion for Rome.
Elizabeth Helman Minchilli

ADDITIONAL PHOTOGRAPHS

FRONT COVER: *The view from a terrace apartment in central Rome takes in the sweeping Spanish Steps.*
BACK COVER: *Fresco from Palazzo del Drago.* PAGE 1: *The dining room of an apartment designed by Andrea Truglio in Rome's Parioli neighbourhood.* PAGES 2/3: *View of Rome from Gianicolo Hill.* PAGE 4: *An eighteenth-century carving at the Palazzo del Drago.* PAGE 6: *Statue of King Vittorio Emanuele II atop the Vittoriano memorial inaugurated in his honour in 1911, now a monument to the Unknown Soldier.* PAGE 8: *A rare Egyptian-style fresco in the Palazzo Massimo alle Colonne, the sixteenth-century palace of the Massimo family.* PAGE 44: *First Empire chair with carved, giltwood chimera, in the salon of Villa Bonaparte.* PAGE 90: *Ceiling detail from the early Renaissance Villa Madama.* PAGE 136: *Mosaic in the Casina di Pio IV, a grotto in the Vatican gardens.* PAGE 176: *The vaulted ceiling of the Galleria in Villa Bonaparte.* PAGE 215: *Fresco detail from Villa Gangalandi.*